Surviving The In-Between

M.M. Bylo

© 2023 by M.M. Bylo

All rights reserved. No part of this book may be reproduced or used in any manner without written permission of the copyright owner except for the use of quotations in a book review. To request permission, contact the copyright owner at marissabylo@gmail.com

All Scripture quotations from the Holy Bible.
© NIV: International Bible Society, 1973.
© TPT: BroadStreet® Publishing Group, 2017.

Printed in the United States of America
First edition, March 2023
Second edition, September 2025

Cover design by Cheyenne van Langevelde
www.thedancingbardess.com

ISBN: 979-8-218-09780-6 (paperback)

www.mmbylo.com
marissabylo@gmail.com

For the dreamers.

Dreams are worth fighting for.
Some you may have to bury.
But they are the seeds for something greater.

"Those who sow with tears will reap with songs of joy.
Those who go out weeping, carrying seed to sow, will
return with songs of joy, carrying sheaves with them."
Psalms 126:5-6

Contents

Part 1: The Real World

2	Moving Out
4	Little Women In The City
5	Mardi Gras
6	Stanley
7	Favorite Things
8	Growing Pains
9	Compromise
10	My Muse Since 2014
11	My Anchor, His Wings
12	In His Arms
13	God Gave Me A Man
14	As For Me
15	The Vow
16	"Quirky"
17	Bloodline
18	Betty
19	Barely Millennial
20	The Question, The Excuse
21	Unqualified
22	Toxic Perseverance
23	Optimistic Confliction
24	Sandcastle Self-Esteem
25	Insecurity's Delusions
26	Funhouse Mirror Shenanigans
27	Dead Weight
28	If Manifesting Works, I Want A Refund
29	Corporate Cop Out
30	I'm Crying In the Bathroom Of A Law Firm
31	A Dream Deferred: Defined
32	Chasing Pavements
33	Pity, Party Of Two
34	Free-Will Prodigal
35	Lost

36	Wilderness Revelations
37	They Encouraged Me To Externally Process (So I Wrote This Instead)
38	Twenty-Four

Part 2: Unprecedented Times

40	Foreshadow (Because Hindsight Is 20/20)
41	2020-isms
42	March 14, 2020
43	Society-Mandated Quarantine
44	Cruel Summer
45	Virtuous Signaling
46	Playing God
47	Hostile Negotiations
48	To What End
49	The Briefest History Lesson
50	Pearls
51	Burning Coals
52	10-42
53	Mask Up (Metaphorically)
54	Smoldering
55	Mountain Getaway Aka Diversion Plan
56	In That Slanted, White Apartment
57	Leave The City
58	Nevertheless, A Reluctant Homecoming
59	Boundaries
60	Status: Critical Condition (Again)
61	Emergency
62	The Last Time I Saw You
64	Iron Sharpens Iron But A Fool's Friend Suffers
65	Sever
66	Come Home, Orphaned Soul
68	Copycat
69	Anti-Hero's Lament
70	Immiscible
71	Twenty-Five

Part 3: Changed For The Better

73	Allegory Of An Actress
75	The Happy Extrovert
77	The Effortless Achiever
78	The Selfless Helper
80	Take A Bow
81	Identity Crisis
82	Quiet Quitting
83	Employed By Hope
84	Little Woman In The Woods
86	To My Younger Self, An Apology
87	Margaret
89	Torchbearers
90	When I Say I Have Panic On Speed Dial
91	I Am A Woman, Not God
92	Far More Than Rubies
93	Falling Scales
94	Beloved
95	The Greatest
96	Invitation
97	Twenty-Six

Part 4: Dropout

99	Scarcity's Anthem
100	Productivity Junkie
101	The Faults Of Ambition
102	Same Old, Same Old
103	Hustle Culture Dropout
104	Mirage
105	Memento Vivere
106	Detour
107	Adamant Gratitude
108	Needlepoint

Part 5: Crumbling Castles

- 110 Chronic Independence
- 111 Burnout 101
- 112 When Sickness Lingers
- 113 Loves Me, Loves Me Not
- 114 Cinderella Retelling (But It's Chronic Illness, Not Magic)
- 115 You Alone Know
- 116 Reconstruction
- 117 Survival Of The Most Stubborn
- 118 Line Leader
- 119 From The Top
- 120 Icicle Eyes
- 121 Twenty-Seven
- 122 Pleasant Places, Someday
- 123 Also By M.M. Bylo & Author Bio

Part 1

The Real World

Moving Out

No one requested this autobiography
But she wrote an unintentional memoir
Brimming with allegories and metaphors
Melancholy but hopeful prose

Let's set the stage
The necessary exposition
This inspired-by-real events transcription
The milestones following adolescence—

Scene One

(The middle of a forest, nowhere story-worthy
Young, little woman, twenty-three
Marrying her high school sweetheart
Witnessed by those who didn't leave)

"Death of a Bachelor" greets the guests
As the groom strolls to a wooden altar
In pearly-white heels and billowing dress
The bride trips along the gravel aisle for a kiss

Twenty One Pilots echoes in the reception hall
As they sway together, man and wife
Her father cuts in for a choreographed dance
A moment she'll forever cherish

An unannounced rainstorm
A wedding gift from God
To compliment the effervescent dance floor
The most expensive, memorable celebration

(The lights dim to darkness)

End of Scene

Scene Two

(Young, little woman speeding along the interstate
To an apartment where her husband awaits
In the outskirts of the inner city
Separated from familiar faces and places)

New city and way of living
Their independence expired
Now a deliberate team of two
They survive whatever the times deliver

Uncertainty hounds her future
A temporary job contract
Job applications multiply to hundreds
As futile college degrees gather dust

The journey of life we are each given
Is never a linear journey
So she boldly steps into the unknown
To find where she belongs

End of Scene.

Little Woman In The City

Naive and doe-eyed
Tentative but trusting
The white picket fences of her childhood
Nowhere to be found

She needed nothing
Once nestled in suburban middle class
Drifting asleep to a train's whistle
As the wind caressed the magnolia flowers

Oblivious of the violence
Stalking innocent souls day and night
The city nearby reaping humans
As they slept to bullet lullabies

Older but perhaps not wiser
Relentless empathy spilling over
She plants herself near the muddy river
Amongst cracked bottles, cigars, and graffiti

Looking up at the frowning monument
A question forming on her lips—
You have something to teach me
I'm not leaving for a while, am I?

Mardi Gras

Bodies stealing more space
Than God created
A plum, emerald, and golden human ocean
Ebb and flow through every city crevice

Makeshift tents and mature day clubs
Bursting at capacity's seams
Overflowing in liquor-saturated secrets
That no one there remembers

Tainted stench and rippling smoke
Greet insatiable noses and mouths
Music pulsating every atom
Laughter, the festivity's heartbeat

I used to envy the merriment
Their happiness roaring in my ears
But is it true and lasting
If it's concocted in pipe or glass?

Stanley

We adore this city
When it's convenient
       Conditionally
Celebrations amassing thousands
For the exalted, inebriated athletes
And their shameless parade on fractured streets

Ignore injustice and poverty
Breathing down our necks
Shrieking for restoration
While you excuse your liter
Escaping home across the river
       What a violent place, you'll say

We don't bleed blue
No, we don't bleed at all.

Favorite Things

A forest-green door eases open
        And closes
Footsteps flatten the shabby, maroon carpet
Crisp Velcro releases
        A bulletproof vest
Calming her morbid ruminations

Television chatter echoes
        Off the twelve-foot ceiling
The screen illuminates anemic walls
        Washed-out, secondhand loveseat
Where two bodies curl into each other
        Safe and sound

The sun bathes tawny bricks
        In rainbow masterpieces
Ivory snowflakes meander
        Along the boulevard
Ivy crawls to meet the azure sky
        Eager for a taste of sunshine…

Growing Pains

Hundreds of silent insect legs
        Creeping along
        Fractured walls
Droning wasp or bee
        Survivors of the manmade outdoors

Rotting wood infested
        With twisted nails
        Haphazardly stacked as balconies and stairs
Glass and plastic bits crunch
        Beneath shoes
The alleyway chokes on power lines

Secondhand smoke floats
        From the hair salon below
Piercing sirens and car horns
        Interrupting thought
Firework or bullet
        The game of questions inevitably played...

Compromise

This city is a conglomerate of feelings
And endless stimuli I can't suppress
I'll take the good, bad, and ugly
As long as he returns home to me.

My Muse Since 2014

Uninspired to write love poems
Yet if the words were lovely
I misunderstood his attention
For the real thing

Give me unrequited feelings
Whatever excuse to hide
A fortress built from heartbreak
My uncomfortable but safe place

Then you came along, unannounced
Revised my schemes for loneliness
You breached my toxic stronghold
To rip out deep-rooted fears

You picked me up
And we danced in its rubble
No one understood the difference
You saw what they couldn't

You ruined me, Darling
But I'm faring well.

My Anchor, His Wings

I rekindle a distant memory—
The first instant I held a boy's hand
And meant the gesture
Sitting in a Dairy Queen parking lot

No concerns or forebodings
My mind ceased spiraling a mere second
How does he slow my tempest thoughts
A magic trick I wasn't taught

The calm before I disclosed dark secrets
And he felt the need to stay
Or at least be prepared
For whenever I crack open again

Because I've spilled out
My heart's torment
Hundreds of moments
Since that frozen February night

Please hold me closer
As ghosts whisper
My deepest regrets and their lies
Demanding for me to listen

But love anchors me
To this dirt
So I don't soar away
Before my time is fulfilled.

In His Arms

Fleeing from hints of love
The instant I discovered an escape
Until I found the safest haven
The calm *after* the storm.

God Gave Me A Man

Who refused to place me on a pedestal
Instead he looked into my eyes
Acknowledged every imperfection
And fiercely loved me
Anyway.

As For Me

Let's forsake this place
And forge our own—
>Where kindness is strength
>Morality is common sense
>Not mere fire insurance

Let them raze the planet
With their frigid bitterness
Stone each other to the ground
In the name of accomplishment
To quench their rigid egos

We'll enjoy our oasis
A kind of palace
We constructed solely for us
And to vex them further—
I'll follow *your* lead.

The Vow

The person standing before you
Is worth more than pure gold
      Accomplishments and ambitions
      Their body you find attractive
      The infectious laughter and grin

Without conditions or expectations
You're accepting past, present, and future
      Flaws and insecurities
      Habits and particularities
They pledge the same in return

Vowing your life to family history
You can't rewrite or overlook
But given an opportunity
To change the future, the ending
As one.

"Quirky"

A creature of habit
Her roots diseased since adolescence
When messages of love and security
Were hijacked by wicked lies

Of course I'm particular
I carry generational baggage
But I can't loosen this grip
I'm not ready yet.

Bloodline

Same coin
Two sides with contrary patterns—
    Anger and sadness
        One spews the pain outward
        The other soaks it into herself

Her tears feel safer than rage
    Than cracked wooden doors
    Than words like bullets
        Aimed and shot
        At those they love

Both choices end the same
Obeying the family commandment—
    Thou shall not emotionally process
Until they throw the generational baggage
Back to hell where it belongs

The choice is theirs—
To let go or pass along.

Betty

Purple pickled beets stain tiny fingertips
Orange spaghetti warming on the stovetop
The baseball game murmurs from an archaic TV

Swing set tucked under a billowing tree
The crunch of autumn leaves below our feet
As a maroon wagon cradles me

Car wheels spinning nowhere on Civic Hill
One wintery afternoon
After elementary school

Your deep pride in my college education
I wish you could have sat in the arena
To watch me cross that stage

A phone call on birthdays
Until you couldn't remember
That disease, a liability to memory

My deepest regret—
Not being there
As you whispered *farewell.*

Barely Millennial

The workplace met me at fifteen
Assistant, cashier, high school actress
Student honors
    But I am *spoiled*
    Anything I want placed in my greedy grasp

Sinking in student loans
Two part-time jobs
Caffeinated anxiety
    But I am *lazy*
    Mindlessly staring at a screen

Thousands of dollars exhausted
My feeble paper diplomas
For charitable business proficiency
    But I am *conceited*
    My sole concern is me

Every generation
    Always worse than the last
        Each passes the torch
            Then blames the next.

The Question, The Excuse

Where were you when
My face met tile, hardwood, carpet
A metal vent molding damp skin
The floor, that loyal floor
Cradling shaking limbs

Sparked in mind then hands and feet
My quaking body begging
Where is the air
As my headphones tell me *I will rise*
But not now, not today

Where were you when
Months of blame ensued
As I examined ceilings for answers
Every *no*, shut door
Prophesying *I am nothing*

My child-like faith tested
As I lay in shambled naivety
The tale of a coward
Conquering the impossible—
Levitating above her worries

Amidst the pity party
Three fingers point back
Accusing me—
Where were you when
They needed a friend

Sorry, I was busy
Crying on the floor.

Unqualified

You know the routine—
    Hundreds of doors
    Meet your nose
    Slamming or latched shut

This brittle paper
Diploma of sweet nothings
Swore fulfilled longings
With fraudulent payoffs

You followed their map and wisdom
Like an obedient hound
Aching teeth and trembling hands
Putting on an act of confidence

The years of tedious work
Morphing to tears soaked up in carpets
Opportunities looming before you
But the doors are bolted

Haunting your ambition
Stalking your infant bravery
Unable to blossom under the weight
Of rejection and setbacks

You do what you've been told—
    Put on that upbeat, charming mask
    And try
    Over and over and over—

Toxic Perseverance

Tell me what's worse—
    A burning impulse to move forward
    Then meet dead ends
        Or a minimal flame
        Avoiding confrontation
        Barely warm enough to stay present

Surely there's a compromise
To pass along this optimism
Ignite a lethargic humanity
In wholesome inspiration
While treading a steady path
Without doubt or distraction

Instead I set my imagination on fire
Then watch that flame dwindle.

Optimistic Confliction

Nothing could stop your determination
Frenzied effort and animated charisma
Becoming materialized dreams

But these brick walls were never your style
An open door much more
To your preference

But now you've tasted the mud
And the fleeing of imagination
Left you rattled and paralyzed.

Sandcastle Self-Esteem

I constructed my confidence
Atop mortal promises and desires
An unreliable foundation

No wonder I crumble
At obstacles and declinations
And quietly stopped trying.

Insecurity's Delusions

I wanted to be someone *important*
Someone who *mattered*
Th *hero* effortlessly saving the realm

Believed I was *so* different
By validating anyone's suffering
Except my own

My dignity shrouded
By talk of good deeds
Instead of action—

Pride's essence
Runs even deeper.

Funhouse Mirror Shenanigans

The sum of me
Is a shunned nuisance
Deemed myself internally flawed
Surely they approve of that self-assessment

Of course I sabotage
Anything I get close to
It's hard to be healthy
When you don't see yourself correctly.

Dead Weight

Wear it like a badge of *dishonor*
A warning, a plea—
      Keep your distance
      No inch of me is worthy

A bad habit
Of loathing my entirety
But you can't reject me
If I never open the door

Please don't notice who I am
But who *you* want me to be
This request hiding the truth—
      Shame lives here with me.

If Manifesting Works, I Want A Refund

I withheld your invitations
To important occasions
But having the audacity
You showed up
And stole the show—

> Laid-back bachelorette parties
> Celebratory reception dinners
> Friend's wedding
> Work ceremonies
> Your presence knows no boundaries

It's degrading energy
But at least I get things done
Productivity, a vain and careless friend
No one can harness anxiety's power
Free of its consequences

I considered you a product
Of unregulated feelings
My blessed but defective childhood
Yet as an adult, full-grown
What am I still running from?

The Corporate Cop Out

Refused to settle until now
I bang my head on this cubicle
Offering dwindling breath to *meaningless*
Wages, benefits, and conversations

Delusional happy hours
And *ceaseless* material perks
Forget passion, my intrinsic motivation
Starving and decaying

Accomplishment is trivial
If purpose hides its face
When creativity and critical thinking
Bow to *mindless* systems

Conformed my path
Submitted to their established footsteps
Ascending an indefinite ladder
Simply, I accepted *less*

So I interrogate my brain—
        What do I want
        And what would assure me
        That I've arrived

I'll tell you if I get there
I'll tell you if I get there.

I'm Crying In The Bathroom Of A Law Firm

And the privilege of that is not lost on me / I'm able to buy necessities or frivolous things / But I don't think I can take another shift / of smashing a keyboard / with wrinkling, paper-cut fingertips / calculating the cost they drained on alcohol / to appease anyone possessing money / Endlessly printing paper / wondering how many forests died / so I can earn an hourly wage / while ignoring complaints / of lake houses and seats to Hamilton / or the clinking of beers on a late Wednesday afternoon.

I don't belong here beside crisp suits and blazers / pretentious cars / midday happy hours / country club memberships and delicate chandeliers / this tax bracket or those who casually dine at the Capital Grille / and the seafood bistro / I don't fit in a sleek, shiny tower staring down at the city below / teeming with adults who can't comprehend why / Beauty and the Beast is my favorite movie / Don't you understand / that appearances fade / Manmade success is temporary / Who cares if you have a castle / but you're not there to enjoy it / beside the one you love / I took my outcast status / found a misunderstood man who loved me better / than an empty mansion ever could / Money might buy happiness / but even that won't linger.

I don't cry from jealousy / These tears speak of something deeper / the disappointment when the heart dreams a dream / that is deferred / time after time.

A Dream Deferred: Defined

1. The slow, sure burial of a dreamer
2. Wistful goodbyes without sympathy cards
3. A silent surrender
4. Forfeit idealizations and passions
5. Forget to dream again.

Chasing Pavements

Pursue aspiration's shadow
But my attempts are futile
A body full of fire
Yet there's no safe place
For the blaze to settle

Hustling to a fault
A dysfunctional try-hard
Lacking expertise and talent
If perseverance counts for something
I'd be a model illustration

This sum of passion
Never equaled
    The rotting fruits of my labor
    Opportunities rigged with fuses
    Trophies without a deeper purpose

My ruminations oscillating
For as long as my memory remembers—
    Is there anywhere on Earth
    For a doubting dreamer
    Such as me?

Pity, Party Of Two

Let's wallow awhile together
Immerse in the depths
Of the heart's disappointments
Melancholy's mire
The thorns of your trial

Your objective's course derailed
That unplanned wave of shock
      Dragged you to bitterness
      Tethered to hopelessness
      Darkened your perspective

How do I simplify this thesis—
Grieve your dream
Bury the absent harvest
Envision a fresh start
Anticipate and build for it

If you can't let go of the past
It will never let go of you.

Free-Will Prodigal

Identify as a daughter
    Of the Most High King
Yes, me, nothing but entitled
    Banished royalty
    Of my own choosing
Begging for scraps
    Of identity and existence
        Among the fickle praise and titles
            Humanity conditionally offers
Ignoring God who rescued me
    From the grave I dug
How memory deceives us
    Surely, I'm flawed from my innermost being
        These clever lies morphed
            My concept of worth
            Into mental ruins
            And I allowed it
Ironic how this turmoil
    Is my handiwork
    My signature design
        That brought disgrace
        And my pursuits to shambles
But I find the audacity
To blame God for all it.

Lost

If good intentions were enough
I would have found my way
Burst through the weeds and briars
To the oasis I envisioned
And devoted years to create

If humanity's wisdom was sufficient
To exclude failure
The road to destiny
Would lay obvious before me
My meet finding level ground

Where am I
The unknown crippled whatever confidence
I grew along the journey
What good are motivation and perseverance
If the map was faulty

With whatever morale I had left
I justified my decisions
Chased the red flags
To a dead end
Only to feel something

My trail guide, my naivety
Truly led us to this wasteland.

Wilderness Revelations

A wayward, stubborn traveler
Trailing a foolish path
Carrying unintended baggage—
    Fear, shame, and regret

No matter if destiny
Lay no further than my fingertips
I can't take hold of it
Until I let these burdens fall away.

They Encouraged Me To Externally Process (So I Wrote This Instead)

I can't deny reality
>	Traveling a twisting trench
>	The crags far above my fingertips
>	Create echo, confusion
>	My inner map grew foggy and silent
>	*Go through or turn around*
>	*Into the unknown or forfeit progress*

I question everything
>	I'm double minded
>	Thrown and tossed by the wind
>	Doubt clutched in shaking fists
>	Help me loosen these stubborn fingers
>	Petrified to believe again
>	Ambition and purpose conflicting

But evermore, I persevere
>	Clinging to encouragement
>	Holy words established
>	Long before I existed
>	The sole strum moving me along—
>	*Take courage*
>	*And press on.*

24

Solitude knocked on my door
In this city of unceasing commotion
If I screamed
Would a soul even stir—
        The reason I am lonely tonight.

Part 2

Unprecedented Times

Foreshadow (Because Hindsight Is 20/20)

They forecasted a storm with high winds
Metal garbage cans reply with slamming lids
And electric wires recklessly swing

> Thunder reverberates through the alleyway
> Like a warning
> *Something is coming*
>
> A gunshot ricochets nearby—
> Just a gun firing into the air
> Not a target, not human flesh
>
> Glass shatters—
> Just feet running across the gravel pavement
> To escape the incoming rain
>
> Smoke escalates in the sky—
> Just the neighbors getting in a final cigarette
> My mind playing catastrophic tricks

I comfort my anxious imagination
Storms don't last forever
But some storms you can't prepare for.

2020-isms

They preach—
In these unprecedented times
We are all in this together

Except for those instructed
To fasten their lips
Shamed for having opinions

I listened with empathy
I smiled with all my teeth
But it's my turn to speak

My perspective that no one asked for
But know when I point a finger
Three curl right back to me.

March 14, 2020

Unfolded as any other evening—
Another party among friends
Where a cat curls up
Next to me
Today we talk about
Working from home
Rather than offices
For a few weeks
The government claims it will
Flatten the curve
Of this raging disease
And we'll comply
It's the right thing to do
Then we laughed
About the confusion
And tension
Waving farewell
I'll see you soon
We promised
Ignorant of
The months
Of separation
That stretched on
Ahead of us.

Society-Mandated Quarantine

Not self-inflicted as tradition has it
But a mandatory isolation
Imposed by government and the public
As civilization collapses into ambiguity

It rids me of positive aspects
That became distractions
From my feelings—
Kin, career, friendship, and my other half

If I can't control much
I'll prescribe myself to self-betterment
Was handed unrestrained time
So I pick up the mirror and paring knife

I evade the negativity
Creeping around the apartment's corners
While I shave off the worthless beliefs
I have of myself

I stay vigilant of the restless clock
As the months sluggishly retire
Talking to myself—
This can't go on forever...right?

Cruel Summer

When universal upheaval turned personal—
>	Furloughed May and June
>	The summer vacation you didn't ask for
>	And unsure if it would end

Local news reports—
>	Food shortage
>	Fifty homicides in July
>	Pillaged, burning buildings

National news laments—
>	Death toll swells
>	Regulations vowing protection
>	Create a conflicting, *new normal*

Each passing month
We remain helpless in our homes
There's little we can do
To alleviate the hurting

How cruel indeed.

Virtuous Signaling

Justly convicted—
> Do I want to *look* good
> Or actually *be* good
Do I seek their recognition
Above doing the *right* thing

I am innocent I plead
But my selflessness boasts strings
Absent actions that would validate
My honey-comb words
Sweet to read but *dead,* nonetheless.

Playing God

Poised on your moral high ground
You declare tolerance for all
While demonizing groups of people
The louder, the better
Attacking their character
Depicting whoever you want as the problem

Wielding cancel culture like a misused mallet
As if thou holier than the rest
Does pinning others' sins
Grant your exclusive righteousness
The self-made moral police
Have you become what you claim to hate

For the equality you preach
Answer this riddle—
When did shame
Accusation, condemnation
And segregation
Ever yield unity and love

Consider the words you speak
And the power that they hold
Life or death hangs on your tongue
Dismount your high horse
Judge your own motives
Don't make this about *you*.

Hostile Negotiations

Shame didn't make me a better person
It failed to embolden me
To help another person
But silenced me instead

Turned me awkward and timid
Serving societal penance
To a black square on the socials
Rather than advocate for change

If an eye for an eye makes the world go blind
Well, my vision is blurry
We murder each other's character
Then expect to find unity

Let's lay our weapons down
Cancel hostility, not each other
For the pitfalls of dishonor, hatred, and pride
Brought us here in the first place.

To What End

Is man's justice
If we are further divided than ever

At least when Jesus
Flipped the temple's tables
He solved the problem.

The Briefest History Lesson

History does not lie—
The system that is broken
Is humanity itself.

Pearls

A Monday night in June
Before the clock struck midnight
The city lit up with burning mortar
Smoke escaping upward
Swells of bodies clashing in chaotic waves
I would have known
If I turned on the local news

Glasses of wine served as a distraction
Huddled in our bed
As if it could shield me
From the lurking pestilence
Even so the faithful sun
Emitted a good report
When it met the blue, smokeless sky

I avoid the details
A vague portrayal
Of a living nightmare
No one has to know
If I disclosed the story
Would they find a way
To invalidate the experience

Instead I hugged him closer
Whispered my woes to moldy apartment walls
While anyone screamed their opinions
No matter who it slandered
I enclosed this memory from the public
Like a traumatic
Wretched secret.

Burning Coals

Have you ever prayed for your enemy
Blessings not curses
Displaying love
Pursue unity
Despite their hostile wishes

Verbal abuse
Hailed at him
Indirectly impaling me
Despised by association
He didn't earn this enmity

They draw an invisible line
You're either on their side or ours
How about consequences for the offender
Not everyone caught in the crossfire
To amend a true wrong

I won't succeed to misplaced anger
Or succumb to the offense
Nothing will drain the mercy out of me
Take the venom elsewhere
This cycle won't persist

Have you ever prayed for your enemy
Blessings without reservations
Because hatred
Never made the world
A better place for anyone.

10-42

The end of the day
Or the end of a *life*
Two outcomes, one coin
Placed in the hands
Of people carrying ill intentions

So what good is weeping
To a siren-saturated evening
I surrendered to sleep while praying
He died as I dreamed
From a shot to his head

Death stalks our frail existence
But the inevitable doesn't warrant
A senseless tragedy
Yet another soul
Stolen without remorse.

Mask Up (Metaphorically)

Is my smirk a battle scar
From years of working customer service
A habitual crutch
Or coping strategy birthed from necessity

I smiled
Through the slander
I smiled
Through hate
Disguised as morality
I smiled
Through nonstop social posts
Landing like a personal attack
I smiled
Resisting the warfare
You ignorantly ignited
In my mind
That wouldn't be won
If I uttered a word

After unceasing grinning
Does your face hurt too?

Smoldering

An emotion stirring at the surface
Such a threatening presence
What a foreign thing
What's its name

Clenched, stubborn jaw
Scorching talons clawing at my chest
Impulsive tears congregate
Behind my eyes

Rippling, control slipping
No instant explosion as expected
But anger all the same
Just give it time

How do I simmer
The seething fury
Before I erupt and incinerate
Anyone in my vicinity?

Mountain Getaway Aka Diversion Plan

The crisp wind and steady sunshine
Momentarily repress
>   Your terror
>   Your anger
>   Your unspoken hurt

Until your lungs forget their job
Gasping on the thin air
And then you'll comprehend—

>   Truly
>   Wildflowers are
>   Unreliable company
>   The trees can't comfort
>   Swaddle you in their limbs
>   Roaming streams deem powerless
>   To lull you into a distracted slumber
>   The stones helpless to stabilize and sooth
> The anger anchored in the bedrock of your soul

Not even the mountains
Can distract you
Detain the pain
You can't utter aloud.

In That Slanted White Apartment

I learned that gunshots don't always occur
In the context you expect
Sirens became my lullaby
Vehicles rumbling like a warning
Of an apocalypse refusing to arrive

A bus stop for ghosts
Of past, present, and future
Failing to keep me
From forgiveness
And eradicating bitterness
Stuck in the roots of my soul

On that slanted black roof
Where I spent several holidays alone
Singing to the rain
Ignoring my pain
Surrounded by looting
And shots fired below

We paid our dues
And finally broke free
Of the white slanted apartment
And its slanted black roof
That city
Alive.

Leave The City

The mental massacre you inflicted
Your locked doors
My pending prayers
And fruitless empathy
Nothing changed here
Except me

Hopelessly optimistic
Surely external efforts
Could help abolish
Centuries of rising violence
But my clamor and good intentions
Can't reconstruct the heart

I wasn't born to fix your precincts
With my powerless striving
A timely lesson from God
I am no one's savior
Or an island lacking resources
But I fought alone

I'll shake the dust off my feet
Drop my baggage at the city limit
When you pursue change
And seize it
For your own sake
I won't claim any credit.

Nevertheless, A Reluctant Homecoming

The train's whistle greets me
As it rumbles along its destined path
That auto body shop still in business
Civic Hill stands proud as ever
But less menacing in the distance

Buildings multiplied over the years
And the trees disappeared
Humans saturating every inch of space
Suburbia granted them
This town a mix of new and old

Some leave here indifferently
Greener grass beckoning
Beyond their comfortable fence
The bait taking them to novel places
To grow, bloom, and stay

I returned to my roots unwillingly
The place God decided
To dig deeper in the dirt
That made me who I am
And who I will be someday.

Boundaries

Are not telling the dental hygienist
Anything
That happened the previous summer
A deadpan smile reassuring her
He's safe
The specific events she mentioned
Occurred years before
Nothing else
And nothing more.

Status: Critical Condition (Again)

More shots fired
But a few blocks
From where we rested our heads
The neighborhood stopped feigning safety

What a useless ploy
A stolen car
Was shooting another human
Worth the petty crime

When does the violence cease
This but a glimpse of what happens
Around this riled Earth
That finds itself in this condition—

Waiting
Groaning
Raging
For some sort of redemption.

Emergency

The substances leading them
To soar above the soil
Mentally
Only to bring them low
Beneath the ground
Stole one too many lives
One soul, too much.

The Last Time I Saw You

Was at a Melanie Martinez concert
Said you were *doing better* and I believed it
We sipped vodka cranberries
Vibed to the musical production
I promised to call after the show
Like I always do

Dreams in the night warned me
To reach back out to you
Instead, always stubborn
I said a prayer that *very* morning
It was already too late
Why is it always too late

But the living have this habit
Death revolves around us
Our grief, our regrets
The should, could, would-haves
Pile as unnecessary weight
And what's left is a remorseful eulogy—

> They described you as a light
> I think I could do better—
> A beacon, a lighthouse
> Providing guidance
> Didn't know a stranger
> Welcoming every soul in your embrace

You taught me I could have opinions
But not couple them with judgment
To speak boldly but include love
Stand for the truth
But honor a person
As they are

My absence wasn't personal
I hid away from the world
To mend my wounds
And after a year I debated
If you'd care to hear from me
I regret it all the time

Tell Jesus I said hi
I'm sure you're telling Him jokes
And He's bent over laughing
We'll talk about Twenty One Pilots
Dissect their lyrics
Concerts I witnessed in your absence

Reminiscence of how we drove four hours
To behold them on a distant stage
But you miraculously touched Tyler's hand
And as he sang our favorite song
In its entirety
We cried along to the melody

Those left behind fixate on memories
It's how we process the heaviness
We'll promise to live better
Not tarry another moment
So I hope you always knew—
You shined the brightest.

Iron Sharpens Iron But A Fool's Friend Suffers

If they celebrate and indulge
In your self-sabotage
The vices stalking your present

They are not your friends
But accomplices
In your self-destruction.

Sever

My deep-rooted wound
An object of my codependency
You despair and I'll save you

But I was never your savior
You could never make me a whole person
Unspoken promises broken long ago

I diagnose it for what we were
Two hurting children
Seeking healing in each other

And if you ever think of me—
I forgave you long ago.

Come Home, Orphaned Soul

Filled with the breath of life
Made in God's image
An inheritance no other creature can claim
But you took this gift
And disowned your place as an heir

A journey to self-made heaven
To live however you desire
But a profound ache
Inherent void you can't simply explain
Followed you to the destination

You searched wherever—
       Father, mother, lover, friend
Seeking an explanation
Returned to your pit empty-handed
Collecting excess scars and trauma

Jaded and battered
You folded inward
Turned to yourself
The true protagonist
The sole meaning of existence

Ran to the ends of the globe
Toiled for a fictional paradise
With every substance, lust, vice
Identity, success, and truth you found
Are they satisfying yet

The answer to your longing—
He's ready to meet you
At the end of your lonely road
To embrace you
And celebrate your return home

What you always wanted
Is still waiting for you.

Copycat

If imitation
Is the sincerest form
Of flattery
Trust me
It's admiration
Turned jealousy
Morphed into deep-rotted envy—
        I want your pleasant personality
        Your charm
        And charisma
        That limitless energy
Your natural ability
To attain goals
And excellent results
        Create artistic pieces
        But purely as a hobby
Your nonchalant intellect
How you spend your seasons
        Engulfed by people
        Who adore you
        Invite you places
        Sing your praises
        A fire that burns that bright

I wasted our allotted time
Wholly wanting to be you
Instead of enjoying friendship
Championing our differences
And cancel my hesitations
Of accepting myself as I am.

Anti-Hero's Lament

I paint myself as the hero
How I rationalize
The skeletons bursting from the closet
And the ghosts nipping at my heels

To those I became a phantom
Leaving you behind
I relied on you noticing my absence
A childish coping mechanism

How do I make progress—
        Do I ask forgiveness
        Do I repair that bridge
But I leave it empty and untraveled

Because silence isn't golden
And regret is the darkest of shades.

Immiscible

Your solitary status
Doesn't mean you're unloved
But silence speaks for itself

No judgment but acceptance
That I cannot control
Their wavering affections

Receiving this lesson—
A part of growing up
May require growing apart

Cherish the severed connection
The deep-rooted memories
Your brain can't dig out

Accept their choices
Lament the separation
Then release them.

25

I used to be terrified of change
Now it's all I'm searching for.

Part 3

Changed For The Better

Allegory Of An Actress

Welcome to my masquerade
What performance
Should I put on
To survive my day

My false identities
Their creator is dysfunction
My favorite acts
Shall I introduce the cast—

The Happy Extrovert
    The heartbeat of the party
    Charisma dripping
    Off her gritted teeth

The Effortless Achiever
    Leads limitless endeavors
    Too wonderful to falter
    Keeps the plates spinning

The Selfless Helper
    Ready to lend a hand
    Anticipating needs
    Poured out for all to drink

Each designed character
Are masters of illusion
Masquerading hypocrites
Contorting to expectations

If the audience enjoys the show
If they like the view
Maybe they will love me
Maybe they won't leave.

The Happy Extrovert

Commence the applause
The life of the party arrives
Laughter, her herald
Announcing her presence
Of exaggerated smile, electric eyes
Her attendance desired here
For what she gives the crowds
She won't object
Their clapping is her salvation

What they fail to notice
The pageant is her escape
Depression lurks like an uninvited guest
Its faithful accomplice, anxiety
Clings to every inch of her
But affirmation and invitations
Delay these frequent villains
And grants her counterfeit peace
Another day in deception

Eventually the lights dim
The music dissipates
And in the quiet of her solitude
The darkness whispers its lies—
Nobody wants to be around a sad person
So she tugs at the strings
Of her mouth
Drags its ends up to the sky
And pretends another night

Afraid of silence
Petrified of stillness
Anticipating the next distraction
Yet she longs for a long-forgotten voice
To break through the hysteria
For in the quiet
If she allows it
He'd remind her of the truth
Warmth saturating every syllable—

You are not defective
Your weakness is not a burden.

The Effortless Achiever

I can't count on anyone but myself
So marvel at her results
The marathons she sprints around everyone
A spotlight fixed on her accomplished facade
And not the pain to preserve it

Aspire to impress the universe
She lost herself in the process
Was shouldering the world's entirety
Worth becoming a shell and machine
For a piece of paper and a handshake

Actions breed consequences
She achieved an image
No longer sustainable—
> The One Who Always Gets It Done
> Independent Woman Who Needs No Help

What a cruel trick of self-sufficiency
She lit her wick at both ends
And expects not to burn out
To shine ever brighter
Inspire the masses forever

Yet a profound longing
Pulls at her wearied heartstrings
For a rest and worth
That's not dependent on her deeds
To hear and believe His promises—

I am enough
You can count on Me.

The Selfless Helper

Say hello to your favorite shadow
She's willing and available
Ready to fill your cup
At the expense of herself

Clinging to *your* pain
Thinking she can save you
Surely her infinite empathy
Is the answer to humanity's suffering

Morality holds her together
There's nothing like using good deeds
As an excuse to hide
To escape the darkness inside her mind

Look closer at her raw hands
A heart cracked open, pleading
Did I do enough for you to love me
Did I do enough to change the world

Her dependency lurking ever deeper—
If I am indispensable
You need me
You can't leave

Yet the good works
Done in her own name
Lay useless and dead
Nothing but spoiled fruit

Amidst the storm of her mind
He whispers to her bleeding heart—
The cosmos doesn't depend on you
You can rest now.

Take A Bow

I've stood on this stage
All my days performing
Painstakingly rehearsed lines
Whatever sounds neat, profound

Standing ovations are my preservation
My A+ performance
Intriguing passing spectators
To stay and humor me

But I tire of pretending
Of the bending and breaking
Merely to be worthy
Of their attention and affection

Wearied of the curated play
This tiring tale I've told
I pull the curtains closed
The onlookers no longer fascinated

I curtsy to the emptied theater
The manipulated lights dim
I rip off the mask and costume
Finally free of the lies.

Identity Crisis

I describe myself as an *underdog*
Because the masses champion
The one who defeats their own giants
Embodying sheer willpower

I've fought an uphill battle
As long as I can remember
But this grasshopper mindset
Anchored me to defeat

Resilience, an admirable trait
The long shot, a misunderstood strength
But *different* is a dangerous label
If I never accept victory.

Quiet Quitting

I surrendered to fear
Lay at the gate of my destiny
My convenient trademark—*incapable*
Because I can't fail
If I don't try

Memorized instances of my inadequacy
In the name of authenticity
    I'll be helpless
    I'll be hopeless
What else do I have to lose

Actually
Everything.

Employed By Hope

To speak the language of victory
I'll tame poison-tipped
Dagger thoughts
Rearrange the critical words
Flowing out my mouth

Remove the labels
I've pinned to my mind
Replace this lens of disappointment—
       That opportunities always end
       In lack and failure

Now I stand at triumph's gate
Adorned for breakthrough
Dwelling in expectation
Eager for forward steps
To live again.

Little Woman In The Woods

A wolf sprints at my heels
Its gnashing teeth
A broken, relentless noise
Pouring from its mouth
What a dreadful howl

A lifetime dedicated to this flight
Vicious chase bred of survival
Led me to a fateful date
I collapsed
Knees scraping against the forest floor

I brace myself to face the monster
The reality I have fled
Yet in lieu of slaughter
The woods fall quiet
As I face the pursuer

There stands a child with bitten nails
Tears pooling in her icicle eyes
Mud smudged across her feet
After saving earthworms from the storms
That sent her to the basement terrified

She matures to a woman
Altered from secular systems
Addicted to movement
Striving to sustain her image
Burning out sooner and sooner

This poisoned, suffering
Version of a character
I constructed to please the masses
To satisfy the scarcity
I chose to focus on

The truth is truly bittersweet—
I was only running from myself.

To My Younger Self, An Apology

Forgiveness is part of the healing journey
So I'm told
I pictured names and instances
Acquitting them repeatedly
Their actions weren't righteous
But I gave it to God
To handle *that* pain

But I neglected an offender
Of those I felt betrayed by—
The child who ignorantly spoke
Hateful words to herself
Grew up in a hurry but acquired emotions
Larger than a young girl could carry
The little one with big feelings

If I could wrap her in a hug
That she would squirm out of
I'd tell her she's *loveable*
Bright, strong
Acceptable
Repeat it again and again
Until her doubts couldn't resuscitate

Please forgive me
I'm so sorry
You were only a little girl
Who wanted to save the world.

Margaret

Pumpkin pies bearing tiny fingermark trenches
Roasted, candied pecans
Greasy chicken thighs and deviled eggs
A gracious host and friend preparing meals
Ready to lend a helping hand

My bestowed middle name
So reverent I couldn't utter it as a kid
Unaware of your story
But now I'm older and grasp
The magnitude you withstood

Facing the brunt of suffering
A man-made soldier
Securing the toughest skin
Resilient spirit, headstrong
Refusing to let go of life

Shielded as much of the agony
A woman could single-handedly handle
But the aftermath created
Sufficient disturbances
That I experienced those aftershocks

I'm forever indebted
To your sacrifices
Safeguarding our generational line
Burning, lingering
In the wake of cruel circumstances

So I'll take the torch
Giving God the traumatic fragments
Patterns of dysfunction
The self-initiated pain and misery
All of that ends with my generation

Take a deep breath—
> My mother's mother's mother
> However far back this goes

You can cry now.

Torchbearers

After decades of vicious battles
We bear our trauma and suffering—
Assured baggage of survival
Nobody leaves without it

Rather we persisted
The lessons learned
The pain endured
Our efforts will not be in vain

We look back at the generations
Developing in our shadows
Letting them make mistakes
But also showing them the way.

When I Say I Have Panic On Speed Dial

It's a custom
For me to call it
Every trigger or buried emotion
Brings me a step closer
To giving anxiety the driver's seat

My nervous imagination
Creating catastrophic figments
Of worst-case scenarios
I still fight it to this day
Panic stays on speed dial
But I don't dial as often

I placed obstacles in panic's way—
>Acknowledgment
>Patience
>Grace
>Mercy
>Healthy coping routines

Though I confess
Mindset intermittently fails
To calm the inevitable tempest
But these habits are a hindrance
Restraining me from dialing
That dreaded tone.

I Am A Woman, Not God

And *thank God*
I don't want the burden
Of humanity
Clutched inside my trembling hands

Humility quickly found me
While I prayed for air
To enter these lungs
They frequently forget how to breathe

I've tasted insecurity and pride
Their fruits are poisonous
I won't let my femininity
Become a deity

I should be respected
        Cherished
        Protected
But I am not God.

Far More Than Rubies

Why should my *body*
Be self-esteem's womb
The source of the world's praise
Showing extra skin never empowered me

Why should a physical form
Be placed on a pedestal
It decays day by day
Nothing buys eternal youth

I'm a beloved temple
But it's not the dwelling
That is worshiped
It's simply a vessel to care for

I obsessed daily
Over my earthly sanctuary
Until I rejected the culture's reverence
And found my worth elsewhere.

Falling Scales

I am no longer apologizing
For these thighs
Or the additional skin
Society demands I despise
To sculpt
Mistreat
And starve

Denying the earthly ritual
Of dissecting myself
Comparison inevitably
Coaxes me to envy
And disrespect
Using shame as a butcher's knife
All in the name of *health*

The scales I stood upon
The hills I climbed
For *thinness's* sake
I passed them with
An indifferent goodbye—
       You don't own me
       And I don't need you anymore.

Beloved

The lie that buried itself
Like a stubborn splinter
Relentless—
    I could disappear
    And no one would notice
I ignore the evidence
That would prove the thesis
As truth

Their affirmation
But deficient sustenance
Naturally unfaithful
A fractured love
I found a source
Of living water quenching
My deepest fears
A fortress, true and stable

No more picking petals off flowers
Demanding their fleeting attention
Searching but never found
Reaching but never held
I am *known*
I am *loved*
By God Almighty
And that is more than enough.

The Greatest

I will love others
Because I was first cherished
By God without conditions

No longer built on mere obligation
Or selfish dependency—
That collapsed the vicious cycle.

Invitation

Since childhood
I wanted to be invited to
The table
Occupied by the trim, tall bodies
Athletic limbs
Charismatic smiles
Brilliant, effortless minds

To belong there, honored and chosen
Waiting for an invite
Into spaces and places
That dismissed people like me
Marked inadequate
A non-disclosed standard
I could never attain

So I prepare my own table
For anyone to join
A limitless guestlist
Everyone is invited
Release your hesitation
No pretending or conditions
Show up as is

Come over and sit with me
Welcome to the family.

26

At last I realized
No one was going to celebrate me
Until I do the same for myself

I denied the pity
And threw
My own party.

Part 4

Dropout

Scarcity's Anthem

Concerns of lack

Everything depends on me

Mistrust my efforts

Strive further

Forsaking rest

Burn out devours my energy

Do I have enough stamina
To power through

I labor evermore

The cycle continues.

Productivity Junkie

Are you dependent on the movement
Does productivity promise you control
Or does it muffle
The clocks in your head
That won't cease their demands

A method that guarantees your survival
Years of chosen chaos
To ace the world's curriculum
Nonstop planning and calculating
You endured it well enough

You braved the free-for-all
Now let the racing of your heart and head
Meet peace and fulfillment
Because in the rush of production
We forgot how to live, didn't we?

The Faults Of Ambition

Doing, having, being
Tailored shoes that take me
To the mountaintop views
But mindful I don't crack the glass ceiling
Never enough or too much—
A contradiction I can't escape

A barbed-wire fence we assembled
This desert we obsess about
Wandering thirsty, begging
See my gold star-worthy credentials
We're far too busy gawking at the mirror
To notice anyone else

Ambition only turns sour
When blinded by vanity
A selfishness stemming soul-deep
When we top off our own glasses
And hoard gifts
Rather than giving to others

What's the point of anything
If we only live for ourselves?

Same Old, Same Old

If happiness was conceived and resided
In man-ordained titles
Pyramids of deeds to touch heaven
And copious happy hours
We would be soaring
But no one notices we're grounded

    We circle the same mountain

I bought the world's lies
Because they sounded nice
And catered to my ego
Infant self-assurance swaddled by conceit
Hoping it could endure
The qualifiers and rejections

    We circle the same mountain again

Spew the same jokes
Same philosophies
Each day a clone of the previous
Does anyone change here
Round and round we go
Complaining and pretending to thrive

    And we circle the same mountain once more.

Hustle Culture Dropout

They assure me
An electronic watch
And its measurements of steps
Create a meaningful journey
Strive until you die, I suppose—

>Earn an emerald lawn
>And pearl picket fence
>Fully furnished four-bedroom house
>Invest in your social circle's envy
>Inspire fruitless competition

>Scale the corporate ladder
>Travel to the ends of the planet
>Tame each inch of bodily blemish
>Fulfill unlimited aspirations
>Even if they aren't your own

>Voted Most—
>>Shiniest person
>>Grandest exterior
>>Most ambitious creature
>>Accomplished *Homo sapien*

But we sink in streaming services
Suffocate in manufactured materials
Flaunting trivial man-made symbols
Bowing to our own temples
Our starving vanity

Whatever this world is offering
I don't want it anymore.

Mirage

I've survived thus far
Then forgot how to live

I've passionately dreamed
But neglected where I am

How do I stop
Seeking the distant future

Without ever enjoying
The present moment?

Memento Vivere

I declined dwelling in the moment
Rather, always glancing back
Relishing in the past
Suffocate in sweet nostalgia
Of departed memories
History looks rosier
In blissful hindsight

Or I stay suspended in a dream
Imagine the near future
Striving for *someday*
That iridescent, perfect horizon
Caressed by my weary grasp
The fruits of my labor
Finally reaped and enjoyed

The present is pain
Torrential feelings I must
Acknowledgement and temper
Reality's expectations are ceaseless
But amidst the demands
There are tiny victories to celebrate
If we could be still and notice

They whisper softly to us—
Remember to live.

Detour

Obsessed with the destination
Maybe I'll stop for once
Take in my surroundings
And enjoy the view.

Adamant Gratitude

I fixated on the finish line
Took for granted the steps in-between
Because it's those strides
These tangible instances
That write our existence
The fleeting time we are given

I'll choose contentment in the face
Of affliction and monotony
What a gift to be appreciated
This present minute
Instead of wishing it aside
To whatever will ultimately arrive

I'll chase the sunsets
Follow the endless horizon
Knowing the impossibility
Wonder is my objective
Finding that effervescent joy
What I truly longed for all along.

Needlepoint

Where's the significance
Of the mess before me
The distinct wreckage
Consequence of my willful decisions

Preoccupied with the finer details
The crisscrossing threads
And obscured picture
How could *this* work out for good

But only You know
The beginning to end
These strings of the chaotic stitching
Holding my days together

Until my final moment
I'll inhale, exhale, and trust
The grand reveal—
Every life is a God-original masterpiece.

Part 5

Crumbling Castles

Chronic Independence

I never needed anyone
Until my knees scraped the ground
My kingdom of flames and ash

My hands outstretched for help
Shame filling in the space between
Once occupied by pride and insecurity

I have myself to thank
That when I sink
No hands are here to catch me.

Burnout 101

I did too much
Racing circles around my peers
Trying harder
Neglecting rest
Until I couldn't quite do
Much of anything.

When Sickness Lingers

No one knows how to react
When *chronic* enters the room
Utter well wishes and health to-do lists
Flippant pity until they stop checking in

Forgot *pushing through* as an option
My body grew vindictive
Intolerant to forward progress
Pain is the payment

I'm not *doing better*
I buried my old ways
And redesigned my will to live
Despite the illness

Don't assume anything about this affliction
Or speak as if I'm not sitting next to you
Imagine if everything you worked for
Was ripped out of your hands

You would be grieving too.

Loves Me, Loves Me Not

The doctors play a guessing game
My symptoms as unreliable clues
    Inconclusive test results
    Adjust medications monthly
    Interrogating misery's source
While normalcy
Is slipping out of my grip
    As ashes nothing more
    Survival mode resurrected

Somedays I'm granted steps, movement
Live as if
    Nothing happened
    Nothing changed
But then I wake up, captive
    To stare endlessly at the ceiling
    Pain forcing me awake
Reminding me I'm alive
Is this living though

Finally learned
To tolerate myself
Now I'll have to discover
How to trust my body again.

Cinderella Retelling (But It's Chronic Illness, Not Magic)

Enveloped within familiar blankets
Prepping my mind for an evening outing
Anticipating certain disturbances and pain
But my body had alternate plans

I'll give you tonight
To laugh and dance with ease
Don't waste your chance
My body implored

Wear the pleated, ruby dress
A loud statement
To the barren, wintery landscape
You always unknowingly beg for attention

Rightfully hesitant but soon surrendering
I spin underneath twinkling lights
No conditions or limitations
Just the music, family, and clumsy feet

I cherished those seconds of freedom
Because sooner than later
That liberty will end—
By midnight it was over.

You Alone Know

A comatose stranger staring off
Vacant eyes devoid of wonder
A shell of who they used to be
Buried their spirited optimism
Along the winding path called life

A depleted skeleton mourning
Everything is meaningless
Powerless to grasp normality
Within its wearied hands
It glanced toward heaven for inspiration

Encourage these barren bones—
    Rattle
    Breathe
    Open my grave
    Live again!

Reconstruction

I ought to rebuild
Reconstruct the remains of my life
But I'm uncertain how
Or where to start.

Survival Of The Most Stubborn

Say hello to my body, the physical mess
My soul's enemy couldn't occupy my mind
He deploys other methods
To trick me in to surrender
To cease the breath in these lungs
The life he's attempted to steal
Since I was born

But the newborn infections
Didn't do their job
The mental bombardment
Didn't hold me down
Discouragement, bitterness
Apathy, and doubt
Relinquished at the foot of a rugged cross

Here's another round
Protecting the days ordained for me
But I have a champion
Battling on my behalf
His strength remedies my weakness
An authority and a winning record
Not even the devil could beat.

Line Leader

My aspirations and plans guaranteed
    Continuous burnout
    An open, coaxing grave
    Eternally striving but ever out of reach

Forsaking wisdom
Dragging You behind me
Pretending You reign over my decisions
While I lord over my life

You gave me what I thought I wanted
But I lived in misery
So my pride reluctantly conceded
I wasn't the woman for the job

Convinced I was so grown up
My character deficiency made it clear—
Even now I shoulder burdens
There's more for me to learn.

From The Top

My Plans
        Expectations
        Motivations
Unraveled before me
I couldn't catch the pieces
Drifting away like smoke
I gather their remains—
Frayed confidence, fatigued empathy

I diligently followed this map
Despite the twists and pitfalls
It circled me back to the start
Years dedicated and spent
Behold a woman less soft
Barring fresh scars
Hands emptied
Of everything I lost

But God presented a choice—
Wallow in pity
Or walk an offbeat path
        A road less traveled
        A call to the wild
Though it tastes like defeat
I have a chance
At a new beginning.

Icicle Eyes

I grieved
My dreams
And lofty ideas
Those that faded away
Or met an early demise

I buried the reality
I thought I wanted
The happy occasions
Pain and misery stole
And those not experienced

I released the people who vanished
Settling inside far-off memories
Those quiet in the ground
And eventually for myself
The woman I was

I gave You my tears in a bottle
Praying they would be the seed
For songs of joy
To burst forth instead
Of weeping.

27

You were
Where you needed to be
All along

Several long years passed
To accept the journey
But you made it nonetheless

God, give us the courage
To walk the path
You created us to live.

Pleasant Places, Someday

I wanted to assure you that I arrived
That the waiting and wandering
Concluded in a happy finale

I haven't seen it yet
But something stirs
Beyond my gaze

It's less about ambition these days
I want to be where God inhabits
The place He called me to settle

I'll need His grace and mercy
Now more than ever
Lead me from this desolate place

Toward green pastures and quiet waters—
I'll tell you about it
When I get there.

Also By M.M. Bylo

<u>Poetry</u>

The Silent Advocate

Through The Long, Dark Night

Not Of This

<u>Novels</u>

University

M.M. Bylo is an author residing in the Midwest with her husband and their rescue cat Luna. Professionally speaking, she has written poetry, short stories, and novellas since the age of ten and minored in Creative Writing in college. In reality, all she dreams about is using her love of storytelling and her own experiences to share the love of Christ and encourage others. You can find her snuggled in blankets and fuzzy socks with a book or video game, wandering the outdoors, or trying to convince her perfectionist brain that rest is productive.

www.ingramcontent.com/pod-product-compliance
Lightning Source LLC
Chambersburg PA
CBHW060327050426
42449CB00011B/2691